By the same author

War in Medieval Society (1974)
Borderland (1984)
Lightning Country (1987)
The King of Ashes (1989)
Clay (1989)
The Confirmation (1992)
Y Felan a Finnau (1992)
The City (1993)
Heroes (1996)
No Hiding Place (1996)
Abergavenny (1997)
The Wine Bird (1998)
Ice (2001)
At the Salt Hotel (2003)
Sea Lilies: Selected Poems 1984-2003 (2006)
The Green Buoy (2006)
Trouble in Heaven (2007)
Tales of the Shopocracy (2009)
West Jutland Suite/Vestjysk Suite (2009)
The Forest Under the Sea (2010)
Fire Drill: Notes on the Twenty-First Century (2010)
A Year of Flowers (2011)
The Roaring Boys (2012)
Footfalls in the Silence (2014)
Wind Playing with a Man's Hat (2016)

Departure Lounge

JOHN BARNIE

Published by Cinnamon Press
Meirion House,
Glan yr afon,
Tanygrisiau
Blaenau Ffestiniog,
Gwynedd,
LL41 3SU
www.cinnamonpress.com

The right of John Barnie to be identified as author of this work has been asserted by him in accordance with the Copyright, Designs and Patent Act, 1988. Copyright © 2018 John Barnie
ISBN:978-1-78864-009-1
British Library Cataloguing in Publication Data. A CIP record for this book can be obtained from the British Library.
All rights reserved. No part of this publication may be reproduced, stored in a retrieval system, or transmitted in any form or by any means, electronic, mechanical, photocopying, recording or otherwise without the prior written permission of the publishers. This book may not be lent, hired out, resold or otherwise disposed of by way of trade in any form of binding or cover other than that in which it is published, without the prior consent of the publishers.

Designed and typeset in Palatino by Cinnamon Press
Original cover design by Adam Craig © Adam Craig

Printed in Poland
Cinnamon Press is represented in the UK by Inpress Ltd www.inpressbooks.co.uk and in Wales by the Welsh Books Council www.cllc.org.uk

Cinnamon Press acknowledges the financial assistance of the Welsh Books Council.

Acknowledgments

Some of these poems first appeared in *At Time's Edge: Remembering Anne Cluysenaar, The New Welsh Review, Planet, Poetry Wales, Red Poets,* and *Starbroek News.*

Contents

Happiness	11
When Darkness Comes	12
Then	13
At the Insect Mausoleum	14
Has Been	15
A Few Words About Mud	16
A Man of the Red Duster	17
Sunday Morning	18
Unusual	19
You Should Try It	20
Ongoing	21
'Black Russian' Tomatoes	22
Approach to the Dark Gates	23
Les and the Girl	24
Neighbours	25
This Wasn't in *The Chronicle*	26
Autopsy	27
A Counter-weight	28
The Glass Lie	29
Isn't It So?	30
Mud, Again	31
Follow Me	32
Conference-Goer	33
Conrad Knew	34
In the Quarry Field	35
Here We Are	36
What Next?	37
Escape	38
Outsourced	39
Think About It	40
Safari!	41
Curriculum Vitae	42
Biology Lesson	43

Wordsworth Is Dead	44
We Thought We Knew Her	45
Hang On	46
Ars Poetica	47
News	48
No One Listened	49
The Minibuses of Guyana	50
At It	51
Again and Again	52
Seldom Seen Now	53
Listening to Mozart	54
Modern Times	55
Crows	56
In Blaenau Ffestiniog	57
Latin for Today	58
'Salem' Revisited	59
The Ruined Farms	60
Mice in the Shed	61
When We Were Young	62
Nature's Home	63
I Like Them, Too	64
Intolerable	65
Spots	66
Conundrum	67
Quick!	68
Bestial	69
A Sunny Day	70
Past It	71
Poets	72
Dark Nights, Now	73
Save Yourselves	74
What Do You Think?	75
How It Is	76

For

Bruce Clunies Ross

&

Anna Marie Degn Nielsen

Departure Lounge

Droll thing life is — that mysterious arrangement of merciless logic for a futile purpose. The most you can hope from it is some knowledge of yourself — that comes too late — a crop of unextinguishable regrets.

       Joseph Conrad, *Heart of Darkness*

Happiness

If you want happiness I'd say it's where
tobogganists slide in a tumble of arms and legs

and there's nothing to do but scream and laugh
as more flakes winnow down

and light fades and crows flag to roost
in the iron branches of the trees.

When Darkness Comes

We had dinner on the lawn last night
and the mountains sat around us and watched,
great beast-like cats waiting for scraps
but of what we never thought to ask;

the poached salmon was delicious
and the apple-pale reflection of the wine danced on the cloth
in the softening rays of the sun

led on the evening's leash, quite tame,
until it slid behind the crags at our back
and cold air descended from rock to rock with its skirmishers,
part of the night's plan of attack.

Then

'My cadaverous rose';
some people would start a poem like that,
not me;
      the first girl I held around the waist
was a Rose, on the brow of the Deri overlooking the town,
her body taut and thin under the summer dress;

withered mountain grass and stone were our seat
where we sat so close our shoulders touched,
each not knowing what to do next, each
pretending my hand wasn't there at the small of her waist,

a breeze ruffling her skirt.

At the Insect Mausoleum

After insects have vanished from the Earth
you'll be glad of the museum's specimens displayed
in boxes with the smell of camphor like a spinster's sheets
pulled up to the chin as a doctor shakes his head;

when did you last see a May bug or a hornet,
the maddening and goading, the crawling and crunched
underfoot; yet even today I saw a tiny fly I've never seen before,
I'm quite sure, under the boughs of an apple tree

where it lived without knowing it existed or had a name
but might be here in one of these boxes displayed and marked
by a Victorian hand that carefully wrote in spindly Latin
whatever it is, genus and species, according to Linné.

Has Been

'Jeg skriver i katakomberna, förstår du' —
           Harry Martinson

I heard he was writing in the catacombs,
but that is a long way underground
and I don't think anyone knew; poets
aren't moles; (I must go, the boosters

are tweeting from the Hall of Fame,
another bard has been shortlisted);
they say he's still there, composing
for his masters the dead; who cares.

A Few Words About Mud

I clear the runnel in the lane, lifting
spadesful of mud into the barrow;

twigs and stones in its mass
are mud growing fists and hair;

mud says there'll be a second coming
and things will settle down as once before;

before prokaryotes?
I upend the barrow and mud

slides into its aeons-old disguise.

A Man of the Red Duster

My cousin sent me the scarecrow sign, 'ninety this year going on ninety-nine'

what remains of flesh on what remains of bone

tapping stick-Morse as he goes about the town

a sailor once on Atlantic convoys, signed on at Newport, Mon, docked at Newport News

Atlantic waves sent the ship in flight until the screws struck air and the hull juddered

then down in a suicidal drop as if to the bottom where hagfish do their work, but no, survived,

signalling now, 'Heavy seas. Big storm approaching. *SS Do or Die*'.

Sunday Morning

The priest does what he can
with transubstantiated bread;

'read my lips'; words
being the chips he bets with

on the Earth's green baize,
croupier mortality raking them in;

'start again' each generation cries,
after their parents' generation dies.

Unusual

An automatic light came on
when a wren snap-darted across the lawn tail up
a feathery flagstaff of itself too quick
each bounce and pounce
for a human eye to follow but no stop
there it is

and gone

You Should Try It

The turbolift will take you to the top of the building in seconds,
it's an amazing thing,
and when the doors go *ping!*
you can step out and see how small we are

the city organised in milling drifts
with *stop!* and *go!*
and fire brigades and ambulances
and people leaning out of windows, wondering how it all began.

Ongoing

Hitler sowed seeds, Germans reaped a harvest,
but it wasn't wheat,
brick after brick the Reich tumbled down,

'hush little baby, don't you cry',
but babies cry, it is their nature;

'where oh where can my true love be'
in a camp, in a ditch;

War has a black-and-white picture it shows around;
'you must do as I did,' it says,
and points to the Middle East's fertile ground.

'Black Russian' Tomatoes

I thought the Black Russians were good,
thunder-clouds massed on an August afternoon
with vile green streaks and inside sullen
off-colour meat you're tempted to sniff,

but plunge in teeth and let the tongue sample
this vegetable butcher's offering that ought
to hang on hooks or be hauled off lorries,
muscled shoulders bearing the vine's weight

of lolling fruit; think of dark rafters, smoky holes,
and you'll be there, ready to savour, 'savour'
being the word Black Russians demand in foreign
gutturals and sweet acidic bloodless juice.

Approach to the Dark Gates

I am trying not to think of how it will be
when history yawns in the library, turning a page,
and a fly buzzes at the window through a long afternoon;

about humanity there's little to say,
'they were here, they stayed a while, their eyes
travelled through space to the stars'.

Les and the Girl

Les was having a bare-foot breakfast when she arrived;
I don't say she sat at his feet,
but I remember his toes
and her auburn hair curling to the waist;

I can't recall what we talked about,
though his poetry for sure;

'I'm a bit of a hair fetishist,' Les said to me once,
and I understood what he meant;

later I heard she was ill, then that she was dead;
I've forgotten her name but not her sitting there,

coppery light tracing through her hair.

Neighbours

She had a frightful fall and that wasn't all,
the doctor said if it goes on like that
she'll have to give up the flat;

it didn't go down well, *I* can tell you;
but as I said, it comes to us all;
'well if *that's* your attitude';

she's changed her will twice,
what a fragile sense of power
shuffling cards

and turning up The Hanged Man;
no, don't stir, I'll see myself out;
you're sure there's nothing I can do;

I'll pop in Tuesday then about half-two;
chin up, stay bright,
ta-ta, ta-ta.

This Wasn't in *The Chronicle*

'Sculpture by Magritte' the Inspector noted, *'Man with Plastic Bag
  for Head'*;
but it was not, it was my old friend dead;

after art had run through the Inspector's mind,
the police procedure proceeded;

when they left, the sun became a red glow
and darkness moved in comfortable among my friend's
  possessions;

just as he knew;
just as he'd said.

Autopsy

The stomach's not as big as you think
slopped in a steel bowl waiting to report
on what went wrong, or rather right;

hands off that staring face under the plastic bag,
death's respirator; swifts are the screaming tearaways
he'll never see again in his grand despair.

A Counter-weight

Snick-snack, the Inspector said,
it was an ordinary do-it-yourself death,
I've seen it before; more interesting
are the jellyfish floating in the harbour
below gently rocking boats, dull

water's daylight pulsing ghosts;
not grace, but peace, before words
brought us tottering to our feet;

this man could have seen them too;

the bag he chose was a 'Bag for Life',
head cocked ironical at the end.

The Glass Lie

We could see through it, yet we believed;
some died for it and had to be buried;
'they did not die in vain'; we believed that too;
summer passed and then it was winter;

we believed in spring, eternal redemption
and the manufacture of bullets; leaders
came and went; one man looked at the glass
and said it was flawed; he was ignored.

Isn't It So

Cleaning the stables was a good idea,
poems rotted down he'd thought were good,

mulch for the garden where broad beans
metamorphose failure into succulence;

it's for the best; walk away free; birds
write nothing but the poems of themselves.

Mud, Again

Mud has no face yet manages a sneer,
how is that? at the edge of a lake once
mud grabbed me by the foot and pulled me down,
my leg disappearing into a sucking shaft;
that'll teach you, I thought it said,
but it couldn't have, could it, mud having no mouth,
just the viciousness that links hands with stars
out in space,

though what is 'in' and what 'out' is hard to say
where dust billows in light-year happenings
that tell us nowhere is central;
mud knew all along of course
and gargles a laugh.

Follow Me

As to the graveyard shuffle,
it's easy, right foot forward, now
the left (lift that slipper, mind that
carpet, watch those stairs);

trees' skirts are flounced by the wind,
birds breed as if it's life or death;

get that walking stick,
tap it to the beat of the weakening heart,
seeing with the clarity of light in water.

Conference Goer

They gave me accreditation;
I was a crab on the sand;

they said 'Would you like to speak';
I hid under a jellyfish;

they said 'There's a buffet';
I filter-fed in the tide;

they said 'Come to the bar';
seaweed never betrayed me;

my manoeuvres were successful;
I left, giving nothing away.

Conrad Knew

Birth is a gift but we don't ask who the giver
is; is it Life, who comes to the table
with fresh bread; or Death who hangs back
in the shadows at the baptism, sharpening
the blade of another day; when the sun goes down
it leaves 'a dark red streak, a long gash inflicted
on the suffering body of the universe'.

In the Quarry Field

You've got to stoop to pick a mushroom
and clutch it gently underneath
to pull it from its tiny grip on earth

while a grey horse comes up nosily
pawing the ground; nothing personal,
it soon wanders off and leaves you

tracking the mushrooms, criss-cross
over the field, joining up haphazard dots,
some master design that might be seen

from the air, the pilot tipping his wings
banking and turning; meanwhile you're there,
morning-shadow Giacometti man;

the stillness in the field is blinding,
the world with one hoof raised, paused,
before the coming of the winter storms.

Here We Are

The cliffs are making a display of broken-down towers
where thrift peers into its little pink purse,

just enough to spend on another summer, it decides,
while bombs fall and the poor, as usual, are driven away.

What Next?

We didn't have typewriters then,
they came in when you were ten;
'that's the end of copperplate,'
Grandfather said and was right;
what next? people flying through air,
Jules Verne trips to the moon; type

isn't the same as a flowing hand,
the dip of a pen in the inkstand,
the patient scratch of a steel nib
across sheets of paper, time to pause
and listen to a blackbird's song
in green gardens after summer rain.

Escape

I had to run out of the museum,
artefacts laid out in cases, explanations,
as if I wanted to know how an adze was used

by hands I never shook;
'oh look'; but I couldn't look;
the polished floorboards sped under me,

the swing doors flashed apart,
and there it was, living people, buses, cars,
the bright habitable world.

Outsourced

There's a smudge on that door
and the ceiling lights need cleaning;
you may be poor but there's more
waiting for a job like this;

don't trip or fall or call in sick;
your earnings are a candle
compared to the glare of ours
in the electronic banks.

Think About It

Imagine a hundred billion galaxies'
dandelion clocks, the seeds their stars,
and a planet where we happen to be
watching the sun rise and go down; dusk

over Cardigan Bay and the Bellevue's
cod and chips, a glass of wine; it's simple;
the soft tread over the carpet to the bar,
to contemplate oneself in its mirrors.

Safari!

Nature, you know, being a dead duck
flung over a hunter's shoulder, we
went on safari; 'living fossils', I called it,
or, 'those-who-are-about-to-die
salute you'; it didn't go down with the wardens;

after a week I'd had enough
bumping and bouncing over red roads;
give me tarmac and gadgets
wherein to see ourselves plain;

hooked thorns of the wait-a-bit
plucked at our sleeves, but not for me
the fading tawny vistas of the past.

Curriculum Vitae

He said he felt 'ill', 'caught in a rut',
but the rut was life,
a winding track he had to travel on,
watering geraniums, lunching with friends,
mowing the lawn, talking to the cat;

that summer he saw one memorable thing,
jellyfish pulsing through limpid water
as if water itself had coalesced in
viscous veils, as if water had come alive
exploring with blind delicacy

what it could mean and why it was there.

Biology Lesson

A finely marked mottle-brown spider
hanging upside down
though perhaps there is no up or down for her

just the elastic dimensions of her web
and readiness to dash
at the slightest touch of a fly

on her trampoline; we
name everything on Earth, but words dissolve,
and there it is again,

a factory of living machines,
a comedy, where beauty mocks us
in its image in a pool of rain.

Wordsworth is Dead

The Earth can't sink, floating in space,
this vivarium where we goggle at the stars
and dream of infesting Mars, 'one day, one day';
until then the vivarium will have to do,

scarred and graffiti'd by our kind,
more the underpass in a giant city
than a traveller reaching an Alpine pass
to gaze on valleys far below.

We Thought We Knew Her

She sent postcards from Interlaken of the '50s kind,
snowbound streets and skiers carrying skis

with red scarves and laughing mouths; we were most impressed,
nobody had done this from our town;

we'd labelled her 'spinster', Victorian times lingering on;
she wrote of 'Franz', the instructor, and 'nursery slopes';

no nursery for her, though; she married late,
happy, we supposed, until he died

and the slide began on the nursery slopes of age,
a last swift slalom rushing up before the smash.

Hang On

Swifts look antiquated now,
the sky's reaping hooks hung in a shed;

even the song of the thrush
is available on-line;

you can't beat machines,
though when we cut ourselves

we wonder why we bleed.

Ars Poetica

More poems that nobody
wants to read; one's failure is
complete; far better respond
to begging letters from Uganda
where life has strength from
being real; the artifice of poetry
sits fishing in a garden pond,
not seeing the heron fishing too
emptying the pond of gold
then flying slowly to its nest.

News

Another mud slide burying a village,
mud the slumberer getting into stride

to push down houses,
drown the poor;

imagine lungs full of mud,
eyes bruised that used to be wells

lovers claimed they drowned in, too,
but not like that.

No One Listened

I'd rather have water than oil, the King said,
and shortly after was found dead, mouth stuffed with gold;

that shows how wise the King was
because oil is the original Philosopher's Stone

that transmutes everything to the one unfathomable precious
    metal,
even the little princes' buckets and spades as they play in the
    desert;

except the prisons—I ought to say that—
where the bars are of steel, and concrete the walls.

The Minibuses of Guyana

*De Sting, Suga Dan, X-Amount, Kevin,
Envious, Ravendra, Rap It Up, De Rock,
Log On, Sancho, De Doctor, Danny Boy*

and here come

*Nicholas 2, Jameer, Ryan, Blessed Child,
Rush Hour, Lisa, Champagne, Sopranos,
Rishi, Indian Chief, Hi-Tech, Tuff Gong*

and more

*Bollywood-GirlsGirlsGirls, Magic Blue,
Hurricane, De Flight, God Bless, Big Head,
Sweet Jesus, Elephant Man, Stampede*

you can take it slow with

*Uncle Robert, Joseph, Nelly, Alvin,
Grace, Touch of Class, Ashley & Kimberley,
Majestic, Play It Safe, White Angel*

or mess with the best

*Fear Dis, Shockin' Vibes, Rapid Fire,
Fully Loaded, Rodman, Big Mac,
Blazer, Cool Dude, De Rhythm, Blast*

whichever you choose, driving down the long coast road,
a warm wind semaphoring in the coconut palms
you will see approaching *D e s t i n y*, the one bus

you cannot refuse.

At It

Clouds floating with intentionless purpose,
waves treading each other down for a glimpse of the land;

birds with dinosauric eyes; fish eyes,
glassy the stare on a fishmonger's slab;

amino acids flung out across space,
do-or-die, the method for creating life;

I'm evolving a theory, in fact one or two;
but I can't tell you yet.

Again and Again

What are the old men doing
munching the past with prosthetic teeth;
paying with coins from the bank of memory
withdrawn from circulation a long time ago;

still, they insist, yes, valid from their point of view
and slapped on the counter as if minted fresh,
yesterday being their tomorrow,
defying us to say otherwise.

Seldom Seen, Now

I'd be with the greenfinches if I could,
the shock of bullion on the wings
which bankers and financiers cannot buy
and can't be coined by human hands;

a Kruger rand chinks when thrown in the street
for others to snaffle and disappear with;
let them go; let them retreat
deeper and deeper into what we are finding

that being human is;
the dance, silhouetted on the hill,
the scythe-man leading, clothes flapping—
that was always the end of the film.

Listening to Mozart

Troubadour butterfly, glimpsed once,
but then it flew by, dancing over the hedge of the years,
to wait on time, summer by summer,

for one more sight; moons come and go
sharp as pollened steel, casting
the Earth into bold sullen shadows, always

still with the stranger muffled and waiting,
but gone by dawn when curtains are drawn back
and an ordinary aspect confronts us again,

because nothing has changed except age
stealthily feeling the heart, except age
stroking the mind in its helmet of bone.

Modern Times

Mechanise me now
before insects inherit the Earth
while galaxies glare
unaware of the tiny enormity
of being here;

take selfies before the operation,
just you and mum,
and if she doesn't survive,
take one at the funeral
by which to remember your grief.

Crows

I like their funeral director style,
their smart can-do with a touch of violence
as they swoop to the lawn for crusts

scattering sparrows;
they only know what they need to know
and were you dead they'd fly down, too,

sizing you up, folding themselves
like black umbrellas
while they strode around.

In Blaenau Ffestiniog

Make a stand beneath the cliffs leaning in over the town
beneath the cloudy swirls of a rainy day
battening and bleak without curiosity; being human

we speak about happiness, rubbing sticks together,
while the rocks gleam blackly under the steady
temptation of the rain to chuck it all in and walk

straight into that unaccountable thing, oblivion.

Latin for Today

I'd write in Latin if I could
but never learned to climb that ivy-covered wall
to find out what's beyond; amo, amas, amat,

porta, porta, portam, machine gun bullets
rattling over a field of corn
where I made a different harvest;

the world's languages, tuned into far away,
twiddling shortwave knobs, ear
pressed close to the woven mesh of the speaker;

but Latin suits me best, so abstract,
a masque for long-dead postulated feelings,
coated in rhetoric.

'Salem' Revisited

La France is a woman, Mam Cymru, too,
pottering about with a chimney for a hat
and a thick woollen shawl,

worrying a saucepan of simmering cawl,
'Duw, the boys will like that';
but France went out and fought for her rights,

built barricades and stormed the prisons;
not for Mam, that nasty violence, 'Ych y fi';
her neighbours are English, their children fill the schools;

'Nid yw Cymru ar werth' never was the rule;
'if the price is right', Mam says, hobbling to capel,
forgetting it's a tyre store, the owner from Liverpool.

The Ruined Farms

I can't help thinking of the ruined farms of the Black Mountains;
 I used to write about them, but can't now, locked out from
 their grey stones and doorless doors;

we've got sheep here, of course, and I can plot the year by the
 lambs and then, suddenly, the empty fields, but I've never
 been to market and seen them penned and sold,

heads over each other's backs while the auctioneer stands legs
 astride, attacked by glossolalia as he edges up the price;
 just as well; the sheep's eyes have a wealth of grass in them,

but nothing more; it's hard to believe the Lady of Sorrows
 doesn't rain down tears from a blue sky, a miracle farmers
 wouldn't understand; it's not going to happen any day soon

as the men with power tools get on with the conquest of
 everything and the farmers go back to the hills to breed more
 sheep, leaving the ruins to themselves.

Mice in the Shed

Little brown Jacks springing from a box,
vanishing tricks I'd disturbed;

I hope they come back
safe from the shadow of the owl,

rags a comfort,
me, the man-ape,

not knowing they were there.

When We Were Young

We set off gaily with a *whoop-whoop* of sirens
and *hip-hip-hoorahs*,
pennants streamed from our masts,
we were going to discover the world;

I met survivors at a funeral,
the blind, led by their daughters,
the red-faced triple-bypass raconteurs,
the ones supported on sticks;

'what happened to—,'
'shipwrecked by his heart on the bedroom floor';

I got into the car that drove us home,
the town nestled in its confluence of valleys
breeding others to shout and roar

till driven back by the tides
to the coffin and the cross.

Nature's Home

title of RSPB magazine

Nature doesn't have a home;
why do we lie to ourselves; there are
shelves, there are vastnesses
seen only by the albatross's eye,
there are caves with slimy walls
and fish like the ghosts of monks,
but nowhere is home; look out,
and what do you see, the passing
of everything; 'my home ain't here'
the old gospel singers sang,
knowing a thing or two;

put another way, there's a hole
in the ground and the pat
of a spade's blade, or just a handy
hedge where an animal lies down
with a flagging heart, a tiny thud
of a bird's body which nobody
hears, an end which nobody sees.

I Like Them, Too

These 'living stones' are more the paw pads of a delicate animal,
timidity come alive and not knowing what to do,
so better hide, stay small, keep still;
if a raindrop now and then plops and rolls off their plain grey
        surface

what a splendour they produce in thrilling gold flowers,
the sun shining upwards from the Earth, not making sense,
though it does to the paw pads that tread in light for several days
softly and gently in the burnt-out glare of the desert.

Intolerable

I'm trying to harden myself and think I'm succeeding;
you see, life bleeds too much at the edges;
I was with my sister-in-law looking for a grave;

we walked around the trim cemetery
and nearly gave up but then I saw it, the name
half hidden by the leaves of a bush; who was it?

not anyone she knew very well, and whoever
had grieved for him had gone their way, the tread of feet
a diminuendo across crunching gravel.

Spots

Turning over in bed I
listened to what the heart
said; Old pump, I replied, I'll
try, just see me through today
while I sit in the conning
tower of the head and work
things out; it did, but did
I; You have too many spots
the heart sighed, like the leopard,
and that I couldn't deny; still
all day the companionable heart
pumped in the soft factory
of the flesh; Hear me out
I said, as I got into bed; see
me through the night; at dawn
I'll try again; the heart made
no reply but pumped to itself
while I slept like the dead.

Conundrum

Truth wriggles under a stone,
desperately small, surprisingly white;
don't leave it exposed to become rotten and die,
thrown out for the bin men;
truth can't be divided
though some say it can and laugh easily if you object
('he's a proper fool');
politicians auction truth,
philosophers twist it into tiny Gordian knots,
looking at the stars;
truth is humble but also proud;
it might live under stones, it says,
but that doesn't mean it is not momentous;
is that true do you think.

Quick!

'Time never runs out but runs on,
and we must, too, planting seeds on newer worlds';

what seeds and what worlds?
'you ask too many questions,

be careful you're not left behind
standing on the shores of nothing but yourself.'

Bestial

We've salted the Earth like Carthage;
one more stick of dynamite says the fisherman throwing it in;
one last crop says the orange farmer drawing water from the
    aquifer;

this motorway will bring prosperity, this high speed train, well,
this high speed train…;
we wake each morning with a billion computers for eyes

but when we are tired and don't sleep too well
and look out of the window at the moon
and wonder about secret goings-on flitting between trees

then it's time to remember Carthage;
the cat took a goldfinch the other day;
no bank would exchange money for its wings.

A Sunny Day

Time burrows deep in my pockets;
I haven't a halfpenny, a farthing of interest;
a slab of ammonites pounded by the sea has more;

I accept this; I have come to realise
humans are small, combing the beach,
grains of sand slipping from our fists.

Past It

He told me of his plans, how he'd bulldoze flat
the moss-covered, boulder-strewn slope behind the house
ridding it of bracken and other weeds,
fell that pine, create a playground for self and guests;

as he spoke I saw Wordsworth,
hand steadying his lean arthritic body
by the stream against a moss-bound oak;
'too old,' he said, 'too old for this now.'

Poets

Leave them alone, I'd say, because
poets aren't worth knowing
plucking at life's sleeve like yourselves

unless diving in pools in unfathomed caves
from which they emerge
with a handful of words they hope will shine.

Dark Nights, Now

How many burnt-out stars are there
in space's coal yards along the way,
never to be humped in sacks over bent backs
by men with leather hoods and capes

to protect them while the cindery stuff
rattles to a stillness in piles in cellars;
how many deep in space, never observed,
impossible to count by astronomers

in endless watch; the mind drifts off,
forgetting the way from the mountain
down to the streets and the sea, dead stars
tagged in the night, but always more;

the palpitating heart in intensive care,
loved ones wandering among the buried
flowers withering on the graves;
how many are there of these burnt-out stars.

Save Yourselves

Christians break bread and say it's Christ's body;
it doesn't mean a thing to swallows
who have gone now, so light in the hand;

nature never shouts Dominus vobiscum;
why should it, self-evolving, self-annihilating;
I, too, am not one for lords or gods.

What Do You Think?

There was a sickle moon this morning
and Venus docking in its arms,
cold, high matter,

and we the anomaly in our twinkling cities,
matter twisting and wriggling, snapping and popping
into thought,

into the unusual fuzzy definition 'I',
the card we lay upon the table, sure
it is trumps.

How It Is

Soon the Earth will be Easter Island
and we its statues' vacant stare;

to pass the time let's start a war
or shoot the last golden oriole;

some say they loved each other,
but they loved the Earth too late.